Practical
Fish Dishes

p^3

This is a P³ Publishing Book
This edition published in 2004

P³ Publishing
Queen Street House
4 Queen Street
Bath BA1 1HE, UK

ISBN: 1-40543-276-4

Printed in China

NOTE

Cup measurements in this book are for American cups.
This book also uses imperial and metric measurements. Follow the same units
of measurement throughout; do not mix imperial and metric.
All spoon measurements are level: teaspoons are assumed to be 5 ml, and
tablespoons are assumed to be 15 ml. Unless otherwise stated,
milk is assumed to be whole milk, eggs and individual vegetables such as potatoes
are medium, and pepper is freshly ground black pepper.

The nutritional information provided for each recipe is per serving or per person.
Optional ingredients, variations, or serving suggestions have
not been included in the calculations. The times given for each recipe are an approximate
guide only because the preparation times may differ according to the techniques used by
different people and the cooking times may vary as a result of the type of oven used.

Recipes using raw or very lightly cooked eggs should be
avoided by infants, the elderly, pregnant women, convalescents,
and anyone suffering from an illness.

Contents

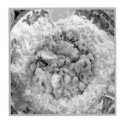

Introduction

Julius Caesar is reputed to have served seafood at banquets, and the oyster and mussel shells that have been found in prehistoric digs show that seafood has always played an important part in everyday diets. Fish continues to grow in popularity for a number of reasons. Nutritionally it meets today's guidelines for healthy eating, it is easy to prepare and cook, and there is now a wide variety available, guaranteed to please everyone's palate.

Types of fish

Fish and shellfish can be divided into a number of categories, as follows.

White fish: these include cod, hoki, halibut, brill, haddock, turbot, flounder, and lemon and Dover sole. All of them contain very little fat and provide an easily digested source of protein, vitamins, and minerals.

Oily fish: this category includes salmon, trout, herring, mackerel, sardines, and pilchards. These fish provide the best sources of omega-3 polyunsaturated fatty acids, which help prevent heart disease and strokes and may help in the prevention of some cancers. Most oily fish are also a good source of the antioxidant mineral selenium.

Crustaceans: these include lobsters, crayfish, shrimp, crabs, and scampi. When plainly cooked, they are a lowfat source of protein and contain the minerals selenium, zinc, and magnesium, as well as some of the B vitamins. Shrimp are high in cholesterol, however, and should be avoided by people watching their cholesterol levels. Crabs contain a significant amount of omega-3 fatty acids.

Molluscs: these include mussels, clams, winkles, whelks, scallops, and oysters. They all contain protein and a certain amount of vitamins, but only traces of minerals. For culinary purposes, other foods such as squid, cuttlefish, octopus, snails, and frogs' legs are included in this category.

Smoked fish: this group includes kippers, smoked mackerel, haddock, trout, and salmon. They provide a good source of protein and B vitamins.

Choosing fish

Always buy fish from a reputable source that has a high turnover, to ensure the freshest fish possible. Whole fish should have bright, clear eyes, and bright red or pink gills. There should be no acrid, ammonia smell—the fish should smell of the sea and the flesh should look firm, not floppy. Frozen fish is often very fresh because it is usually caught and processed at sea.

If buying raw oysters, mussels, or clams, the shells should be closed, or should close when tapped lightly. Discard any with damaged shells.

Storing fish

Fresh fish and shellfish should be consumed within 1-2 days. Refrigerate as soon as possible after purchase.

Because of the risk of food poisoning, you should store and prepare shellfish with great care. Keep raw mussels, clams, and oysters in the refrigerator, either tightly wrapped in damp newspaper or covered with cold water in a large bowl. Soaking the shellfish helps to clean them prior to cooking.

If freezing fresh fish, ensure it is fresh, and clean it first. Wrap well in freezer wrap, label clearly, and freeze on the day of purchase. Most fish start to deteriorate after 3 months of freezing. If you are buying frozen fish, freeze

it as soon as possible after purchase. NEVER refreeze frozen fish that has started to thaw. Thaw it thoroughly in the refrigerator before cooking.

Fish techniques

Fish dealers and staff working at supermarket fish counters are usually willing to prepare fish for you, but at busy times you may have to wait, so it is useful to know how to clean and fillet fish for yourself.

Scaling fish: place the fish on a counter. Working from the tail end, scrape away the scales with a round-bladed, blunt knife, working your way up to the head. When finished, thoroughly rinse the fish.

Cleaning fish: for round fish, such as herring, mackerel, and trout, slit the fish along the belly toward the gills. Carefully scrape out the entrails, then thoroughly rinse in cold water. Cut off all the fins, and the gills, which are located just under the head. If preferred, cut off the head; if leaving the head on, many people prefer to remove the eyes. For flat fish, such as flounder and sole, place the fish, dark side up, on a counter and make a slit behind the gills. Scrape out the entrails and cut off the fins, then wash thoroughly in cold water.

Skinning fish: to skin whole round fish, make a slit around the head, loosen the skin on one side, then pull sharply down toward the tail. Turn the fish over and repeat. To skin flat fish, start with the dark side up. Make a slit above the tail, loosen the skin, pull sharply toward the head, and cut off. The white skin is often left on, but if you wish to remove it, turn the fish over and repeat.

Filleting fish: for round fish, remove the head and cut along the backbone. Carefully ease the flesh from the bone as you work down to the tail end, then cut off from the tail. Turn the fish over and repeat. For flat fish, place the fish, dark side up, on a counter and cut along the backbone from head to tail. Make a cut below the head, following the line of the fish. Gently ease the knife into the fish so that it is on the bone, then work the knife

along, easing off the flesh. Lift the fillet off, then repeat with the other side. Use the trimmings from filleting and skinning fish to make fish bouillon (see below).

Boning cooked fish: once the fish is cooked, place it on a counter and, if necessary, carefully peel away the skin. Cut the bone at the head and tail, insert a knife between the flesh and bone, and gently ease off the flesh. Once the bone is exposed, it can be removed. If boning fish to be decorated before serving, such as whole salmon, snip the bone at the tail and head with a pair of scissors. Carefully slip a knife along the length of the backbone, gently easing the flesh off the bone. Very carefully pull out the bone, and decorate as desired.

Fish bouillon

You can buy fresh fish bouillon from many stores, but it is often expensive. You can also buy it in cube form, although these can be very salty. Making your own bouillon is easy, quick, and produces a superior result in any dish.

To make your own bouillon, use any fish trimmings that you have, or ask your fish dealer for any leftover trimmings. Skin, gills, bones, and heads are ideal. Place 1 lb 9 oz/700 g fish trimmings in a large pan with 1 small chopped onion, 1 chopped carrot, 1 chopped celery stalk, 6 peppercorns, 1 fresh bouquet garni, and 2 strips of thinly pared lemon rind. Cover with cold water and bring to a boil. Skim off any scum that floats to the surface, lower the heat, cover with a lid, and simmer gently for 30 minutes. Let cool, strain, and refrigerate for up to 2 days. If you wish to keep it for longer, freeze in ice-cube trays, then pack in heavy-duty freezer bags, label, and store. Use within 2-3 months.

KEY

 Simplicity level 1–3 (1 easiest, 3 slightly harder)

 Preparation time

 Cooking time

Thai-Style Seafood Soup

Since taste and tolerance for chiles vary, using chili puree instead of fresh chiles offers more control of the heat.

NUTRITIONAL INFORMATION	
Calories 132	Sugars 7g
Protein 20g	Fat 2g
Carbohydrate 9g	Saturates 0g

  10 mins   20 mins

SERVES 4

I N G R E D I E N T S

5 cups fish bouillon

1 lemongrass stalk, split lengthwise

pared rind of ½ lime or 1 lime leaf

1-inch/2.5-cm piece of fresh gingerroot, sliced

¼ tsp chili puree

4–6 scallions, sliced

7 oz/200 g large or medium raw shrimp, peeled and deveined

9 oz/250 g scallops (about 16–20)

2 tbsp fresh cilantro leaves

salt

finely chopped red bell pepper or fresh red chile rings, to garnish

VARIATION

Substitute very small baby leeks, slivered or thinly sliced diagonally, for the scallions. Include the green parts.

1 Put the bouillon in a pan with the lemongrass, lime rind or lime leaf, ginger, and chili puree. Bring just to a boil, lower the heat, cover, and simmer for 10–15 minutes.

2 Cut the scallions in half lengthwise, then slice crosswise very thinly. Cut the shrimp almost in half lengthwise, keeping the tails intact.

3 Strain the bouillon, return to the pan, and bring to a gentle simmer. Add the scallions and cook for 2–3 minutes. Taste and season with salt, if needed, and stir in a little more chili puree, if desired.

4 Add the scallops and shrimp and poach for about 1 minute, until they turn opaque and the shrimp curl.

5 Add the cilantro leaves, ladle the soup into warmed bowls, and garnish with red bell pepper or red chile rings.

Crab & Cabbage Soup

From the Vera Cruz region of Mexico, this delicious soup uses fresh crab meat to add a rich flavor to a mildly spicy vegetable and fish broth.

NUTRITIONAL INFORMATION

Calories 131	Sugars 10g
Protein 13g	Fat 4g
Carbohydrate . . .12g	Saturates 0g

25 mins   35 mins

SERVES 4

I N G R E D I E N T S

¼ cabbage

1 lb/450 g ripe tomatoes

4 cups fish bouillon or boiling water mixed with 1–2 fish bouillon cubes

1 onion, thinly sliced

1 small carrot, diced

4 garlic cloves, finely chopped

6 tbsp chopped fresh cilantro

1 tsp mild chili powder

1 whole cooked crab or 6–8 oz/175–225 g crab meat

1 tbsp torn fresh oregano leaves

salt and pepper

TO SERVE

1–2 limes, cut into wedges

salsa of your choice

1 Cut out and discard any thick stalks from the cabbage, then shred the leaves finely using a large knife.

2 To skin the tomatoes, place in a heatproof bowl, pour boiling water over to cover, and let stand for about 30 seconds. Drain and plunge into cold water. The skins will then slide off easily. Coarsely chop the skinned tomatoes.

3 Place the tomatoes and bouillon in a pan with the onion, carrot, cabbage, garlic, fresh cilantro, and chili powder. Bring to a boil, then lower the heat and simmer for about 20 minutes, until the vegetables are just tender.

4 If using whole crab, remove the crab meat. Twist off the legs and claws and crack with a heavy knife. Remove the flesh from the legs with a skewer; leave the cracked claws intact, if desired. Remove the body section from the main crab shell and remove the meat, discarding the stomach sac and feathery gills that lie along each side of the body.

5 Add the crab meat and oregano leaves to the pan and simmer for 10–15 minutes to combine the flavors. Season to taste with salt and pepper.

6 Ladle into deep soup bowls and serve immediately with 1–2 wedges of lime, per serving. Hand around a bowl of your chosen salsa separately.

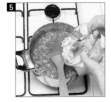

Smoked Haddock Soup

Smoked haddock gives this soup a marvelously rich flavor, while the mashed potatoes and cream thicken and enrich the bouillon.

NUTRITIONAL INFORMATION

Calories	169	Sugars	.........8g
Protein	........16g	Fat	...........5g
Carbohydrate	...16g	Saturates	......3g

 25 mins   40 mins

SERVES 4–6

I N G R E D I E N T S

8 oz/225 g smoked haddock fillet

1 onion, finely chopped

1 garlic clove, crushed

2½ cups water

2½ cups skim milk

2⅔–4 cups hot mashed potatoes

2 tbsp butter

about 1 tbsp lemon juice

6 tbsp lowfat plain yogurt

4 tbsp chopped fresh parsley

salt and pepper

1 Put the fish, onion, garlic, and water into a pan. Bring to a boil, cover, and simmer over low heat for about 15–20 minutes.

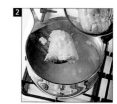

2 Remove the fish from the pan. Strip off the skin and remove all the bones, and reserve both. Flake the flesh finely with a fork.

3 Return the skin and bones to the cooking liquid and simmer for 10 minutes. Strain, discarding the skin and bones. Pour the cooking liquid into a clean pan.

4 Add the milk and flaked fish and season to taste with salt and pepper. Bring to a boil and simmer for about 3 minutes.

5 Gradually whisk in sufficient mashed potato to give a fairly thick soup, then stir in the butter and sharpen to taste with lemon juice.

6 Add the yogurt and 3 tablespoons of the chopped parsley. Reheat gently and adjust the seasoning, if necessary. Sprinkle with the remaining parsley and serve the soup immediately.

COOK'S TIP

Undyed smoked haddock may be used in place of the bright yellow fish; it will give a paler color, but just as much flavor. Alternatively, use smoked cod or smoked whiting.

Provençal Fish Soup

For the best results, you need to use flavorful fish, such as cod or haddock, for this recipe. Frozen fish fillets are also suitable.

NUTRITIONAL INFORMATION

Calories ......122 Sugars 6g
Protein ....12g Fat 3g
Carbohydrate ....7g Saturates 0g

10 mins   1½ hrs

SERVES 4–6

INGREDIENTS

1 tbsp olive oil

2 onions, finely chopped

1 small leek, thinly sliced

1 small carrot, finely chopped

1 celery stalk, finely chopped

1 small fennel bulb, finely
   chopped (optional)

3 garlic cloves, finely chopped

scant 1 cup dry white wine

14 oz/400 g canned tomatoes

1 bay leaf

pinch of fennel seeds

2 strips of orange rind

¼ tsp saffron threads

5 cups water

12 oz/350 g white fish fillets, skinned

salt and pepper

croûtons, to serve (optional)

2 Add the wine and simmer for 1 minute. Add the tomatoes, bay leaf, fennel seeds, orange rind, saffron, and water. Bring just to a boil, lower the heat, cover, and simmer gently, stirring occasionally, for 30 minutes.

3 Add the fish and cook for another 20–30 minutes, until it flakes easily. Remove the bay leaf and orange rind.

4 Remove the pan from the heat and set aside to cool slightly, then transfer to

a blender or food processor and process to a smooth puree, working in batches if necessary. (If using a food processor, strain off the cooking liquid and reserve. Puree the soup solids with enough cooking liquid to moisten them, then combine with the remaining liquid.)

5 Return the soup to the pan. Taste and adjust the seasoning, if necessary, and simmer for 5–10 minutes, until heated through. Ladle the soup into warmed bowls and sprinkle with croûtons, if using. Serve.

1 Heat the oil in a large pan over medium heat. Add the onions and cook, stirring occasionally, for about 5 minutes, until softened. Add the leek, carrot, celery, fennel, if using, and garlic, and continue cooking for 4–5 minutes, until the leek is wilted.

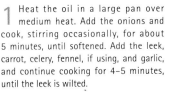  

Thai Seafood Salad

This colorful mixture of vegetables, topped with succulent seafood and tossed in a piquant dressing, is best served chilled.

NUTRITIONAL INFORMATION

Calories	310	Sugars	.........4g
Protein	........30g	Fat	..........18g
Carbohydrate	....7g	Saturates	.......3g

1¼ hrs   10 mins

SERVES 4

INGREDIENTS

1 lb/450 g live mussels, scrubbed

8 jumbo shrimp

12 oz/350 g prepared squid, sliced into rings

4 oz/115 g peeled cooked shrimp

½ red onion, thinly sliced

2 cups bean sprouts

½ red bell pepper, seeded and sliced

4 oz/115 g bok choy, shredded

DRESSING

1 garlic clove, crushed

1 tsp grated fresh gingerroot

1 red chile, seeded and finely chopped

2 tbsp chopped fresh cilantro

1 tbsp lime juice

1 tsp finely grated lime rind

1 tbsp light soy sauce

5 tbsp sunflower or peanut oil

2 tsp sesame oil

salt and pepper

1 Place the mussels in a large pan with just the water that clings to the shells. Cook over high heat for 3–4 minutes, shaking the pan occasionally, until they have opened. Discard any that remain closed. Strain, reserve the liquid, and refresh under cold water. Drain again.

2 Bring the reserved liquid to a boil and simmer the jumbo shrimp for 5 minutes. Add the squid and cook for another 2 minutes. Remove them with a slotted spoon and plunge into a large bowl of cold water. Reserve the poaching liquid. Drain the shrimp and squid again.

3 Remove the mussels from their shells and mix with the jumbo shrimp, squid, and peeled shrimp. Chill for 1 hour.

4 Put all the dressing ingredients, except the oils, into a blender and blend to a smooth paste. Add the oils, reserved poaching liquid, seasoning, and 4 tablespoons of cold water. Blend again.

5 Combine all the vegetables and toss with 2–3 tablespoons of the dressing. Transfer to a large serving plate. Toss the seafood with the remaining dressing and add to the vegetables. Serve immediately.

Lobster & Avocado Salad

This isn't really an entrée but would serve very well as a light lunch with some bread or as part of a buffet.

🄖 🄖

🥪 25 mins   🕐 3 mins

SERVES 4

I N G R E D I E N T S

two 14-oz/400-g cooked lobsters

1 large avocado

1 tbsp lemon juice

8 oz/225 g green beans

4 scallions, thinly sliced

2 tbsp chopped fresh chervil

1 tbsp chopped fresh chives

D R E S S I N G

1 garlic clove, crushed

1 tsp Dijon mustard

pinch of sugar

1 tbsp balsamic vinegar

5 tbsp olive oil

salt and pepper

1 To prepare the lobsters, cut them in half lengthwise. Remove the intestinal vein that runs down the tail, the stomach sac, and any gray beards from the body cavity at the head end of the lobster. Crack the claws and remove the meat—in one piece if possible. Remove the meat from the tail of the lobster. Coarsely chop all the meat and set aside.

2 Split the avocado lengthwise and remove the pit. Cut each half in half again and peel off the skin. Cut the avocado flesh into chunks and toss with the lemon juice to prevent it from discoloring. Add to the lobster meat.

3 Bring a large pan of lightly salted water to a boil and add the green beans. Cook for 3 minutes, then drain, and immediately refresh under cold water. Drain again and set aside to cool completely. Cut the beans in half, then add them to the avocado and lobster.

4 Meanwhile, make the dressing by whisking together the garlic, mustard, sugar, vinegar, and seasoning. Gradually add the oil, whisking, until thickened.

5 Add the scallions, chervil, and chives to the lobster and avocado mixture and toss gently together. Drizzle over the dressing and serve immediately.

Lentil & Tuna Salad

In this recipe, lentils combined with spices, lemon juice and tuna make a marvelously tasty and filling salad.

NUTRITIONAL INFORMATION

Calories	227	Sugars	........2g
Protein	........19g	Fat	..........9g
Carbohydrate	...19g	Saturates	.......1g

25 mins   0 mins

SERVES 4

INGREDIENTS

2 ripe tomatoes

1 small red onion

3 tbsp extra-virgin olive oil

1 tbsp lemon juice

1 tsp whole-grain mustard

1 garlic clove, crushed

½ tsp ground cumin

½ tsp ground coriander

14 oz/400 g canned lentils, drained

6½ oz/185 g canned tuna, drained

2 tbsp chopped fresh cilantro

pepper

1 Using a sharp knife, seed the tomatoes and then chop them into small cubes. Finely chop the red onion.

COOK'S TIP

Lentils are an excellent source of protein and contain several important vitamins and minerals. Buy them dried for soaking and cooking yourself, or buy canned varieties for speed and convenience.

2 To make the dressing, whisk together the olive oil, lemon juice, mustard, garlic, cumin, and ground coriander in a small bowl, until thoroughly combined. Set aside until required.

3 Mix together the chopped onion, diced tomatoes, and drained lentils in a large bowl.

4 Flake the tuna with a fork and stir it into the onion, tomato, and lentil mixture. Stir in the chopped fresh cilantro and mix well.

5 Pour the dressing over the lentil and tuna salad and season with pepper to taste. Serve immediately.

Smoked Mackerel Pâté

This is a quick and easy pâté with plenty of flavor. It originates in Goa, on the west coast of India, an area famous for its seafood.

NUTRITIONAL INFORMATION

Calories	316	Sugars	.........3g
Protein	........13g	Fat	..........23g
Carbohydrate	...14g	Saturates	.......8g

 4 hrs   5 mins

SERVES 4

I N G R E D I E N T S

7 oz/200 g smoked mackerel fillet

1 small, fresh, green chile, seeded and chopped

1 garlic clove, chopped

3 tbsp fresh cilantro leaves

⅔ cup sour cream

1 small red onion, chopped

2 tbsp lime juice

salt and pepper

4 slices white bread, crusts removed

1 Skin and flake the mackerel fillet, removing any small bones. Put the flesh in the bowl of a food processor with the chile, garlic, cilantro, and sour cream. Process until smooth.

2 Transfer the mixture to a bowl and mix in the onion and lime juice. Season to taste with salt and pepper. The pâté will seem very soft at this stage, but will firm up in the refrigerator. Cover with plastic wrap and chill for several hours, or overnight if possible.

3 To make Melba toasts, place the trimmed bread slices under a preheated medium broiler and toast lightly on both sides. Using a long, sharp knife, split the toasts in half horizontally, then cut each across diagonally to form 4 triangles per slice.

4 Put the triangles, untoasted side up, under the broiler and toast until golden and curled at the edges. Serve the Melba toast warm or cold with the smoked mackerel pâté.

COOK'S TIP
This pâté is also very good served with crudités.

Japanese Sushi

These little snacks are made with special seasoned rice and a variety of toppings. Sushi rice is available from Japanese foodstores.

NUTRITIONAL INFORMATION

Calories 403	Sugars 6g
Protein 24g	Fat 8g
Carbohydrate . . .56g	Saturates 1g

1 hr   30 mins

SERVES 4–6

I N G R E D I E N T S

14 oz/400 g sushi rice

generous 2 cups water

4 tbsp Japanese rice vinegar

1½ tbsp superfine sugar

1½ tsp salt

1½ tbsp mirin (Japanese rice wine)

N O R I M A K I   S U S H I

2 eggs

pinch of ground turmeric

1–2 tbsp vegetable oil

4 sheets dried nori seaweed

4 oz/115 g smoked salmon slices, cut into 3-inch/7.5-cm pieces

½ cucumber, lightly peeled, cut into fourths, seeded, then thinly sliced lengthwise

fresh chives

N I G I R I   S U S H I

16 cooked peeled shrimp

wasabi paste (Japanese horseradish)

3 oz/85 g smoked salmon fillet, cut into ¼-inch/5-mm slices

sesame seeds, lightly toasted

T O   S E R V E

pickled ginger

Japanese soy sauce

  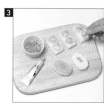

1 Put the rice and water in a pan and bring to a boil. Cover and simmer for 20 minutes. Set aside for 10 minutes. Bring the vinegar, sugar, salt, and mirin to a boil. Pour the mixture evenly over the surface of the rice and blend in, fanning the rice at the same time.

2 For the norimaki sushi, beat the eggs with the turmeric and 1 teaspoon of the oil, then make 2 omelets and cook them in the remaining oil. Cut them in half. Pass the sheets of nori over a flame for a few minutes to toast. Lay a piece of nori, toasted side down, on a sushi mat. Lay an omelet half on top, leaving a border. Spread over a thin layer of sushi rice. Place a piece of smoked salmon on the bottom third of the rice, trimming to fit, and top with cucumber and chives. Moisten the border of the nori with water and roll up. Repeat with the rest and let set. Cut into 1-inch/2.5-cm slices, cover, and chill.

3 For the nigiri sushi, using wet hands, shape 2 tablespoons of the rice at a time into ovals. Top with 2 shrimp or a dab of wasabi and some smoked salmon. Sprinkle with the sesame seeds. Serve the sushi with the pickled ginger and soy sauce.

Salmon Pancakes

These pancakes are based on the latke, which is a thin, crisp pancake, and are served with smoked salmon and sour cream for a taste of luxury.

NUTRITIONAL INFORMATION

Calories	142	Sugars	.........1g
Protein	........6.8g	Fat	..........7.8g
Carbohydrate	..11.9g	Saturates	.....2.8g

5 mins   25 mins

SERVES 4

I N G R E D I E N T S

1 lb/450 g mealy potatoes, peeled and grated

2 scallions, chopped

2 tbsp self-rising flour

2 eggs, beaten

2 tbsp vegetable oil

salt and pepper

fresh chives, to garnish

T O P P I N G

⅔ cup sour cream

4½ oz/125 g smoked salmon

1 Rinse the grated potatoes under cold running water, drain, and pat dry on paper towels. Transfer to a mixing bowl.

2 Mix the scallions, flour, and eggs into the potatoes and season well with salt and pepper.

3 Heat 1 tablespoon of the vegetable oil in a heavy skillet. Drop about 4 tablespoons of the mixture into the skillet and spread each one with the back of a spoon to form a circle (the mixture should make 16 pancakes). Cook for about 5–7 minutes, turning once, until golden. Drain well.

4 Heat the remaining oil and cook the remaining mixture in batches.

5 Top the pancakes with the sour cream and smoked salmon, garnish with fresh chives, and serve hot.

VARIATION
These pancakes are equally delicious topped with prosciutto or any other dry-cured ham instead of the smoked salmon.

Giant Garlic Shrimp

In Spain, giant garlic shrimp are cooked in small, half-glazed earthenware dishes called "cazuelas." The shrimp arrive at your table sizzling.

NUTRITIONAL INFORMATION

Calories	385	Sugars	.........0g
Protein	........26g	Fat	..........31g
Carbohydrate	....1g	Saturates	.......5g

 5 mins   5–8 mins

SERVES 4

I N G R E D I E N T S

½ cup olive oil

4 garlic cloves, finely chopped

2 hot, fresh, red chiles, seeded and
finely chopped

1 lb/450 g cooked jumbo shrimp

2 tbsp chopped fresh flatleaf parsley

salt and pepper

lemon wedges, to garnish

crusty bread, to serve

1 Heat the olive oil in a large, heavy-
bottomed skillet over low heat. Add
the garlic and chiles and cook, stirring
occasionally, for 1–2 minutes, until
softened but not colored.

2 Add the shrimp and stir-fry for
2–3 minutes, until heated through
and coated in the oil and garlic mixture.

3 Turn off the heat and add the
chopped fresh flatleaf parsley, stirring
well to mix. Season to taste with salt
and pepper.

4 Divide the shrimp and garlic-flavored
oil among warmed serving dishes and
serve with lots of crusty bread. Garnish
with lemon wedges.

COOK'S TIP

If you can get hold of raw
shrimp, cook them as above,
but increase the cooking time to
5–6 minutes, until the shrimp are
cooked through and bright pink. If
using frozen shrimp, make sure they
are thoroughly thawed before cooking.

Provençal Mussels

This recipe conjures up the flavors of southern France—tomatoes, wine, herbs, and garlic combine to make a tasty mussel stew.

NUTRITIONAL INFORMATION

Calories 194	Sugars 5g	
Protein 12g	Fat 10g	
Carbohydrate 9g	Saturates 2g	

🦞 10 mins   🕐 1¼ hrs

SERVES 4

I N G R E D I E N T S

2 lb/900 g live mussels

3 tbsp olive oil

1 onion, finely chopped

3 garlic cloves, finely chopped

2 tsp fresh thyme leaves

⅔ cup red wine

1 lb 12 oz/800 g canned chopped tomatoes

2 tbsp chopped fresh parsley

salt and pepper

crusty bread, to serve

1 Clean the mussels by scrubbing or scraping the shells and pulling out any beards. Discard any mussels with broken shells or any that do not close when tapped sharply. Put the mussels in a large pan with just the water that clings to their shells. Cover and cook over high heat, vigorously shaking the pan occasionally, for 3–4 minutes, until all the mussels have opened. Discard any mussels that remain closed. Drain, straining and reserving the cooking liquid. Set aside.

2 Heat the oil in a large pan and add the onion. Cook over low heat for 8–10 minutes, until softened but not colored. Add the garlic and thyme and cook for another minute. Add the wine and simmer rapidly, until reduced and syrupy. Add the tomatoes and the mussel cooking liquid. Bring to a boil, cover, and simmer for 30 minutes. Uncover the pan and cook for another 15 minutes.

3 Add the mussels and cook for another 5 minutes, until heated through. Stir in the parsley, season to taste with salt and pepper, and serve with plenty of fresh crusty bread.

VARIATION

Replace the mussels with an equal quantity of clams.

Corsican Clam Spaghetti

Fresh mussels can also be used to make this simple but delicious pasta sauce. Serve with a glass of chilled white wine.

NUTRITIONAL INFORMATION			
Calories	550	Sugars	........10g
Protein	........25g	Fat	..........16g
Carbohydrate	...82g	Saturates	.......2g

 50 mins 25 mins

SERVES 4

INGREDIENTS

14 oz/400 g dried or fresh spaghetti

salt and pepper

CORSICAN CLAM SAUCE

2 lb/900 g live clams

4 tbsp olive oil

3 large garlic cloves, crushed

pinch of dried chili flakes (optional)

2 lb/900 g tomatoes, skinned and chopped, with juice reserved

½ cup green or black olives, pitted and chopped

1 tbsp chopped fresh oregano or ½ tsp dried oregano

1 Place the clams in a bowl of lightly salted water and set aside to soak for 30 minutes. Rinse them under cold, running water and scrub lightly to remove any sand from the shells.

2 Discard any broken clams or open clams that do not shut when firmly tapped with the handle of a knife. This indicates they are dead and could cause food poisoning if eaten. Set the clams aside to soak in a large bowl of water. Meanwhile, bring a large pan of lightly salted water to a boil.

3 Heat the oil in a large skillet over medium heat. Add the garlic and chili flakes, if using, and cook, stirring constantly, for about 2 minutes.

4 Stir in the tomatoes, olives, and oregano. Lower the heat and simmer, stirring frequently, until the tomatoes soften and start to break up. Cover and simmer for 10 minutes.

5 Meanwhile, add the spaghetti to the pan of boiling water, bring back to a boil, and cook until tender, but still firm to

the bite (8–10 minutes for dried spaghetti and 4–5 minutes for fresh). Drain well, reserving about ½ cup of the cooking water. Keep the pasta warm.

6 Add the clams and reserved cooking liquid to the sauce and season to taste. Bring to a boil, stirring constantly. Discard any clams that have not opened and transfer the sauce to a larger pan.

7 Add the pasta to the sauce and toss until well coated. Transfer the pasta to individual dishes. Serve immediately.

Seafood Lasagna

You can use any fish and any sauce you like in this recipe—
try smoked haddock and whiskey sauce, or cod with cheese sauce.

NUTRITIONAL INFORMATION

Calories ....790 Sugars 23g
Protein ....55g Fat 32g
Carbohydrate ...74g Saturates 19g

 30 mins   45 mins

SERVES 4

I N G R E D I E N T S

1 lb/450 g smoked haddock fillet, skin
   removed and flesh flaked

4 oz/115 g shrimp

4 oz/115 g sole fillet, skin removed and
   flesh sliced

juice of 1 lemon

4 tbsp butter

3 leeks, very thinly sliced

6 tbsp all-purpose flour

about 2½ cups milk

2 tbsp honey

1¾ cups grated mozzarella cheese

1 lb/450 g precooked lasagna

⅔ cup freshly grated Parmesan cheese

pepper

1 Put the haddock fillet, shrimp, and sole fillet into a large bowl and season with pepper and lemon juice to taste. Set aside while you make the sauce.

2 Melt the butter in a large pan. Add the leeks and cook over low heat, stirring occasionally, for 8 minutes, until softened. Add the flour and cook, stirring constantly, for 1 minute. Gradually stir in enough milk to make a smooth, thick, creamy sauce.

3 Blend in the honey and mozzarella cheese and cook for another 3 minutes. Turn off the heat and mix in the fish and shrimp.

4 Make alternate layers of fish sauce and lasagna in a casserole, finishing with a layer of fish sauce on top. Generously sprinkle over the grated Parmesan cheese and bake in a preheated oven, 350°F/180°C, for 30 minutes. Serve immediately.

VARIATION

For a cider sauce, substitute 1 finely chopped shallot for the leeks, 1¼ cups hard cider and 1¼ cups heavy cream for the milk, and 1 teaspoon mustard for the honey. For a Tuscan sauce, substitute 1 chopped fennel bulb for the leeks and omit the honey.

Linguine with Sardines

This is a very quick dish that is ideal for midweek suppers because it is so simple to prepare, but is packed full of flavor.

NUTRITIONAL INFORMATION

Calories	547	Sugars 5g
Protein	. . . . .23g	Fat 23g
Carbohydrate	. . .68g	Saturates 3g

🔥 10 mins   🕐 12 mins

SERVES 4

I N G R E D I E N T S

8 sardines, filleted

1 fennel bulb

4 tbsp olive oil

3 garlic cloves, sliced

1 tsp chili flakes

12 oz/350 g dried linguine

½ tsp finely grated lemon rind

1 tbsp lemon juice

2 tbsp pine nuts, toasted

2 tbsp chopped fresh parsley

salt and pepper

COOK'S TIP

Reserve a couple of tablespoons of the pasta cooking water and add to the pasta with the sauce if the mixture seems a little dry.

1 Wash the sardine fillets and pat dry on paper towels. Cut them into large pieces and set aside. Trim the fennel bulb and slice very thinly.

2 Heat 2 tablespoons of the olive oil in a large, heavy skillet and add the garlic and chili flakes. Cook for 1 minute, then add the fennel slices. Cook over medium-high heat, stirring occasionally, for 4–5 minutes, until softened. Lower the heat, add the sardine pieces, and cook for another 3–4 minutes, until just cooked.

3 Meanwhile, bring a pan of lightly salted water to a boil. Add the pasta, bring back to a boil, and cook for about 8–10 minutes, until tender but still firm to the bite. Drain well and return to the pan.

4 Add the lemon rind, lemon juice, pine nuts, and parsley to the sardines and toss together. Season to taste with salt and pepper. Add to the pasta with the remaining olive oil and toss together gently. Transfer to a warmed serving dish and serve immediately.

Jambalaya

Jambalaya is a dish of Cajun origin. There are as many versions of this dish as there are people who cook it. Here is a straightforward one.

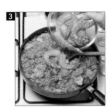

NUTRITIONAL INFORMATION

Calories	283	Sugars	.........8g
Protein	........30g	Fat	..........14g
Carbohydrate	...12g	Saturates	.......3g

 10 mins   45 mins

SERVES 4

I N G R E D I E N T S

2 tbsp vegetable oil

2 onions, coarsely chopped

1 green bell pepper, seeded and
    coarsely chopped

2 celery stalks, coarsely chopped

3 garlic cloves, finely chopped

2 tsp paprika

10½ oz/300 g skinless, boneless chicken
    breast portions, chopped

3½ oz/100 g kabanos sausages, chopped

3 tomatoes, skinned and chopped

2¼ cups long-grain rice

3¾ cups hot chicken or fish bouillon

1 tsp dried oregano

2 bay leaves

12 large shrimp tails

4 scallions, finely chopped

2 tbsp chopped fresh parsley

salt and pepper

salad, to serve

1 Heat the vegetable oil in a large skillet and add the onions, bell pepper, celery, and garlic. Cook over low heat, stirring occasionally, for about 8–10 minutes, until all the vegetables have softened. Add the paprika and cook for another 30 seconds. Add the chicken and sausages and cook for 8–10 minutes, until lightly browned. Add the tomatoes and cook for 2–3 minutes, until softened.

2 Add the rice to the pan and stir well. Pour in the hot bouillon and stir in the oregano and bay leaves. Cover and simmer for 10 minutes over very low heat.

3 Add the shrimp and stir well. Cover again and then cook for another 6–8 minutes, until the rice is tender and the shrimp are cooked through.

4 Stir in the scallions and parsley and season to taste. Serve with salad.

COOK'S TIP

Jambalaya is a versatile dish, which has some basic ingredients— onions, green bell peppers, celery, rice, and seasonings. You can add whatever else you have at hand.

Seafood Rice

This satisfying rice casserole, bursting with Mediterranean flavors, can be made with any combination of seafood you choose.

NUTRITIONAL INFORMATION

Calories 571   Sugars 18g
Protein . . . . .25g   Fat 16g
Carbohydrate . . .81g   Saturates 3g

15 mins   1 hr

SERVES 4–6

I N G R E D I E N T S

4 tbsp olive oil

16 large, raw, peeled shrimp

8 oz/225 g cleaned squid, sliced

2 green bell peppers, seeded and cut
lengthwise into ½-inch/1-cm strips

1 large onion, finely chopped

4 garlic cloves, finely chopped

2 bay leaves

1 tsp saffron threads

½ tsp dried crushed chilies

3½ cups risotto rice or Valencia rice

1 cup dry white wine

3¾ cups fish, chicken, or
vegetable bouillon

12–16 littleneck clams, well scrubbed

12–16 large mussels, well scrubbed

salt and pepper

2 tbsp chopped fresh flatleaf parsley

B E L L   P E P P E R   S A U C E

2–3 tbsp olive oil

2 onions, finely chopped

4–6 garlic cloves, finely chopped

4–6 roasted red bell peppers in olive oil

14 oz/400 g canned chopped tomatoes

1–1½ tsp hot paprika

salt

1 To make the bell pepper sauce, heat the oil in a pan. Add the onions and cook for 6–8 minutes, until golden. Stir in the garlic and cook for 1 minute. Add the remaining ingredients and simmer gently, stirring occasionally, for about 10 minutes. Process in a food processor to a smooth sauce. Set aside and keep warm.

2 Heat half the oil in a wide pan over high heat. Add the shrimp and stir-fry for 2 minutes, until pink. Transfer to a plate. Add the squid and stir-fry for about 2 minutes, until just firm. Set aside with the shrimp.

3 Heat the remaining oil in the pan, add the green bell peppers and onion and stir-fry for about 6 minutes, until just tender. Stir in the garlic, bay leaves, saffron, and chilies and cook for 30 seconds. Add the rice and cook, stirring constantly, until thoroughly coated.

4 Add the wine and stir until absorbed. Add the bouillon and season to taste with salt and pepper. Bring to a boil and cover. Simmer gently for about 20 minutes, until the rice is just tender and the liquid is almost absorbed.

5 Add the clams and mussels. Replace the cover and cook for 10 minutes, until the shells open. Discard any that remain closed. Stir in the shrimp and squid. Replace the cover and heat through. Sprinkle with the chopped parsley and serve immediately with the sauce.

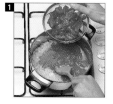

Haddock Baked in Yogurt

This is a very simple, convenient, flavorsome dish, which uses mainly pantry ingredients—apart from the fresh fish.

NUTRITIONAL INFORMATION

Calories	448	Sugars	........16g
Protein	........47g	Fat	..........21g
Carbohydrate	...20g	Saturates	.......8g

🕑 20 mins   ⏱ 40 mins

SERVES 4

I N G R E D I E N T S

2 large onions, thinly sliced

2 lb/900 g haddock fillet

scant 2 cups plain yogurt

2 tbsp lemon juice

1 tsp sugar

2 tsp ground cumin

2 tsp ground coriander

pinch of garam masala

pinch of cayenne pepper

1 tsp grated fresh gingerroot

3 tbsp vegetable oil

¼ cup cold unsalted butter, diced

salt and pepper

freshly cooked snow peas, to serve

1 Line the bottom of a large casserole with the onion slices. Cut the fish widthwise into strips about 2 inches/5 cm wide and lay the strips in a single layer over the onions.

2 In a bowl, combine the yogurt, lemon juice, sugar, cumin, coriander, garam masala, cayenne, ginger, and oil and season to taste with salt and pepper. Pour this sauce over the fish, tipping the dish to make sure it runs under the fish as well. Cover tightly with kitchen foil or a lid.

3 Bake in a preheated oven, 375°F/190°C, for 30 minutes, or until the fish is just tender.

4 Carefully pour the sauce off the fish into a pan. Bring to a boil over low heat and simmer to reduce to about 1½ cups. Remove from the heat.

5 Add the cubes of butter to the sauce and whisk until melted and fully incorporated. Pour the sauce over the fish and serve with freshly cooked snow peas.

COOK'S TIP

When you pour the sauce off the fish it will look thin and separated, but reducing and stirring in the butter will help to amalgamate it.

Fish & Chips

This is the genuine British fish and chips: crunchy, golden batter surrounding perfectly cooked cod, served with golden crispy fries.

NUTRITIONAL INFORMATION

Calories 1191   Sugars 4g
Protein . . . . .44g   Fat 76g
Carbohydrate . . .84g   Saturates 10g

 1¾ hrs   30–35 mins

SERVES 4

I N G R E D I E N T S

vegetable oil, for deep-frying

2 lb/900 g potatoes

four 6-oz/175-g pieces of cod fillet

salt and pepper

B A T T E R

½ oz/15 g fresh yeast

1¼ cups beer

2 cups all-purpose flour

2 tsp salt

M A Y O N N A I S E

1 egg yolk

1 tsp wholegrain mustard

1 tbsp lemon juice

1 cup light olive oil

salt and pepper

T O   G A R N I S H

lemon wedges

sprigs of fresh parsley

1 For the batter, cream the yeast with a little beer. Gradually stir in the remaining beer. Sift the flour and salt into a bowl, make a well in the center, and whisk in the yeast. Cover and leave at room temperature for 1 hour.

2 For the mayonnaise, blend the egg yolk, mustard, lemon juice, and seasoning in a food processor for 30 seconds, until frothy. Gradually add the olive oil, in a slow, steady stream, until incorporated. Season. Thin with a little hot water if it is too thick. Refrigerate until needed.

3 Peel the potatoes and cut into chips ½ inch/1 cm thick. Heat a large pan half-filled with vegetable oil to 275°F/140°C, or until a cube of bread browns in 1 minute. Cook the chips in 2 batches for 5 minutes, until cooked but not browned. Drain on paper towels and set aside.

4 Increase the heat to 325°F/160°C, or until a cube of bread browns in 45 seconds. Season the fish, then dip in the batter. Cook 2 pieces at a time for 7–8 minutes, until golden. Drain on paper towels and keep warm.

5 Increase the heat to 375°F/190°C, or until a bread cube browns in 30 seconds. Cook the chips again, in 2 batches, for 2–3 minutes, until golden. Drain on paper towels and sprinkle with salt. Garnish the fish and chips with lemon wedges and parsley. Serve with mayonnaise.

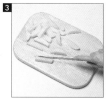

Stuffed Mackerel

This is an easier variation of a Middle Eastern recipe for stuffed mackerel, which involves removing the mackerel flesh while leaving the skin intact.

NUTRITIONAL INFORMATION

Calories	488	Sugars	........12g
Protein	........34g	Fat	..........34g
Carbohydrate	...12g	Saturates	.......6g

10 mins

20 mins

SERVES 4

INGREDIENTS

4 large mackerel, cleaned

1 tbsp olive oil

1 small onion, thinly sliced

1 tsp ground cinnamon

½ tsp ground ginger

2 tbsp raisins

2 tbsp pine nuts, toasted

8 grape leaves in brine, drained

salt and pepper

VARIATION

This stuffing works equally well with many other fish, including sea bass and red snapper.

1 Wash the fish, pat dry with paper towels, and set aside. Heat the oil in a small skillet and add the onion. Cook gently for 5 minutes, until softened. Add the cinnamon and ginger and cook for 30 seconds, then add the raisins and pine nuts. Season to taste. Remove from the heat and let cool.

2 Stuff each fish with one-fourth of the stuffing mixture. Wrap each fish in 2 grape leaves, securing with toothpicks.

3 Cook on a preheated barbecue or ridged grill pan for 5 minutes on each side, until the grape leaves have scorched and the fish is tender.

Tilapia en Papillote

The beauty of this dish is that the fish cooks with a selection of vegetables, so you need only cook some boiled new potatoes to serve with it.

NUTRITIONAL INFORMATION

Calories	368	Sugars	.........2g
Protein	........49g	Fat	..........18g
Carbohydrate	....3g	Saturates	.......3g

 10 mins   15 mins

SERVES 4

INGREDIENTS

2 tilapia, filleted

1 cup pitted black olives

12 cherry tomatoes, halved

4 oz/115 g green beans

handful of fresh basil leaves

4 fresh lemon slices

4 tsp olive oil

salt and pepper

fresh basil leaves, to garnish

boiled new potatoes, to serve

1 Wash and dry the fish fillets and set aside. Cut 4 large rectangles of baking parchment measuring about 18 x 12 inches/46 x 30 cm. Fold in half to give a 9 x 12-inch/23 x 30-cm rectangle. Cut this into a large heart shape and open it out.

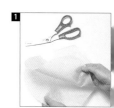

2 Lay 1 tilapia fillet on 1 half of the parchment heart. Top with one-fourth of the olives, tomatoes, green beans, and basil, and 1 lemon slice. Drizzle over 1 teaspoon of olive oil and season to taste with salt and pepper.

3 Fold over the other half of the parchment and fold the edges of the parchment together to enclose. Repeat this process to make 4 packages.

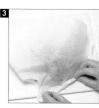

4 Place the packages on a cookie sheet and cook in a preheated oven, 400°F/200°C, for about 15 minutes, or until the fish is tender.

5 Transfer each package to a serving plate, unopened, letting your guests open their packages and enjoy the marvelous aromas. Suggest that they garnish their portions with fresh basil and serve with a generous helping of boiled new potatoes.

VARIATIONS

Try spreading the fish with a little olive paste, some chopped sun-dried tomatoes, a little goat cheese, and fresh basil.

8

Whole Sea Bass with Ginger

This is a lovely Asian-inspired dish of sea bass, delicately flavored with scallions, ginger, and soy sauce.

NUTRITIONAL INFORMATION	
Calories 185	Sugars 1g
Protein 31g	Fat 6g
Carbohydrate 2g	Saturates 1g

🔺 10 mins   🕐 15 mins

SERVES 4

INGREDIENTS

1 lb 12 oz/800 g whole sea bass, cleaned and scaled

4 tbsp light soy sauce

5 scallions, cut into long, fine shreds

2 tbsp finely shredded fresh gingerroot

4 tbsp fresh cilantro leaves

5 tsp sunflower oil

1 tsp sesame oil

4 tbsp hot fish bouillon

lime wedges, to garnish

steamed rice, to serve

1 Wash the fish and pat dry with paper towels. Brush all over with 2 tablespoons of the soy sauce. Sprinkle half the scallions and all the ginger over a steaming tray or large plate and put the fish on top.

2 Half fill a large pan with water and fit a steamer on top. Bring the water to a boil. Put the steaming plate with the sea bass into the steamer and cover with a tight-fitting lid. Keeping the water boiling, steam the fish for 10–12 minutes, until tender and cooked through.

3 Carefully remove the plate and lift the fish onto a serving platter, leaving behind the scallions and ginger. Scatter over the remaining scallions and fresh cilantro leaves.

4 Put the sunflower oil into a small pan and heat until almost smoking. Add the sesame oil and immediately pour the hot oils over the fish and scallions. Mix the remaining soy sauce with the fish bouillon and pour this over the fish. Garnish with lime wedges and serve immediately with steamed rice.

Hake Steaks with Chermoula

The cooking time may seem long and indeed you could decrease it slightly if you prefer, but in Morocco they like their fish well cooked!

NUTRITIONAL INFORMATION

Calories	590	Sugars	.........1g
Protein	........42g	Fat	..........46g
Carbohydrate	....2g	Saturates	.......7g

1¼ hrs   35–40 mins

SERVES 4

I N G R E D I E N T S

4 hake steaks, about 8 oz/225 g each

1 cup pitted green olives

freshly cooked vegetables, to serve

M A R I N A D E

6 tbsp finely chopped fresh cilantro

6 tbsp finely chopped fresh parsley

6 garlic cloves, crushed

1 tbsp ground cumin

1 tsp ground coriander

1 tbsp paprika

pinch of cayenne pepper

⅔ cup fresh lemon juice

1¼ cups olive oil

VARIATION

Remove the fish from the marinade and dust with seasoned flour. Cook in oil or clarified butter, until golden. Warm the marinade, but do not boil, and serve as a sauce with lemon slices.

1 For the marinade, combine the fresh cilantro, parsley, garlic, cumin, ground coriander, paprika, cayenne, lemon juice, and olive oil in a bowl.

2 Wash the hake steaks and pat dry with paper towels. Place them in a casserole. Pour the marinade over the fish and set aside for at least 1 hour, and preferably overnight.

3 Before cooking, sprinkle the olives over the fish. Cover the dish with foil.

4 Cook in a preheated oven, 325°F/ 160°C, for 35–40 minutes, until the fish is tender. Serve immediately with freshly cooked vegetables.

Sole Florentine

This is a classic combination of rolled sole fillets in a creamy cheese sauce cooked with spinach. You can make the cheese sauce in advance.

NUTRITIONAL INFORMATION

Calories	945	Sugars	........12g
Protein	........80g	Fat	..........59g
Carbohydrate	...23g	Saturates	......32g

45 mins 50 mins

SERVES 4

INGREDIENTS

2½ cups milk

2 strips of lemon rind

2 tsp fresh tarragon

1 bay leaf

½ onion, sliced

2 tbsp butter, plus extra for greasing

4 tbsp all-purpose flour

2 tsp mustard powder

3 tbsp freshly grated Parmesan cheese

1¼ cups heavy cream

pinch of freshly grated nutmeg

1 lb/450 g fresh spinach

four 1 lb 10-oz/750-g Dover soles, quarter-cut fillets (2 from each side of the fish)

salt and pepper

TO SERVE

crisp salad greens

crusty bread

1 Put the milk, lemon rind, tarragon, bay leaf, and onion into a pan and bring to a boil over low heat. Remove from the heat and set aside for 30 minutes for the flavors to steep.

2 Melt the butter in a clean pan and stir in the flour and mustard powder. Strain the steeped milk, discarding the lemon, herbs, and onion. Gradually whisk in the milk, until smooth. Bring to a boil over low heat, stirring constantly, until thickened. Simmer gently for 2 minutes. Remove from the heat and stir in the cheese, cream, nutmeg, and seasoning. Cover the surface with plastic wrap.

3 Grease a large casserole. Blanch the spinach leaves in boiling salted water for 30 seconds. Drain and refresh under cold water. Drain and pat dry. Put the spinach in the bottom of the casserole.

4 Wash and dry the fish fillets. Season and roll up. Arrange on top of the spinach and pour over the cheese sauce. Transfer to a preheated oven, 400°F/200°C, and cook for 35 minutes, until bubbling and golden. Serve immediately with crisp salad greens and crusty bread.

VARIATION

For a budget version of this dish, use lemon sole instead of Dover sole.

Layered Fish & Potato Pie

This is a really delicious and filling dish. Layers of potato slices and mixed fish are cooked in a creamy sauce and topped with grated cheese.

NUTRITIONAL INFORMATION

Calories	116	Sugars	.......1.9g
Protein	........6.2g	Fat	..........6.1g
Carbohydrate	...9.7g	Saturates	.....3.8g

10 mins   55 mins

SERVES 4

I N G R E D I E N T S

2 lb/900 g waxy potatoes, sliced

5 tbsp butter

1 red onion, halved and sliced

5 tbsp all-purpose flour

2 cups milk

⅔ cup heavy cream

8 oz/225 g smoked haddock fillet, cubed

8 oz/225 g cod fillet, cubed

1 red bell pepper, seeded and diced

4 oz/115 g broccoli florets

⅔ cup freshly grated Parmesan cheese

salt and pepper

1 Cook the sliced potatoes in a pan of boiling water for 10 minutes. Drain and set aside.

2 Meanwhile, melt the butter in a pan, add the onion and cook gently for 3–4 minutes.

3 Add the flour and cook for 1 minute. Blend in the milk and cream and bring to a boil, stirring, until the sauce has thickened.

4 Arrange half of the potato slices in the bottom of a shallow casserole.

5 Add the fish, red bell pepper, and broccoli to the sauce and cook over low heat for 10 minutes. Season with salt and pepper, then spoon the mixture over the potatoes in the dish.

6 Arrange the remaining potato slices in a layer over the fish mixture. Sprinkle the Parmesan cheese over the top.

7 Cook in a preheated oven, 350°F/ 180°C, for 30 minutes, or until the potatoes are cooked through and the topping is golden.

 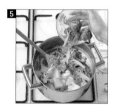 

COOK'S TIP

Choose your favorite combination of fish, adding salmon or various shellfish for special occasions.

Cod Curry

Using curry paste in this recipe makes it quick
and easy to prepare. It makes an ideal family supper.

NUTRITIONAL INFORMATION	
Calories 310	Sugars 4g
Protein 42g	Fat 8g
Carbohydrate ...19g	Saturates 1g

10 mins   25 mins

SERVES 4

I N G R E D I E N T S

1 tbsp vegetable oil

1 small onion, chopped

2 garlic cloves, chopped

1-inch/2.5-cm piece of fresh gingerroot,
coarsely chopped

2 large ripe tomatoes, skinned and
coarsely chopped

⅔ cup fish bouillon

1 tbsp medium curry paste

1 tsp ground coriander

14 oz/400 g canned garbanzo beans,
drained and rinsed

1 lb 10 oz/750 g cod fillet, cut into
large chunks

4 tbsp chopped fresh cilantro

4 tbsp thick yogurt

salt and pepper

steamed basmati rice, to serve

1 Heat the oil in a large pan and add the onion, garlic, and ginger. Cook over low heat for 4–5 minutes, until softened. Remove from the heat. Put the onion mixture into a food processor or blender with the tomatoes and fish bouillon and process until smooth.

2 Return to the pan with the curry paste, ground coriander, and garbanzo beans. Mix together well, then simmer gently for 15 minutes, until thickened.

3 Add the pieces of fish and return to a simmer. Cook for 5 minutes, until the fish is just tender. Remove from the heat and set aside for 2–3 minutes.

4 Stir in the cilantro and yogurt. Season and serve with basmati rice.

VARIATIONS
Instead of cod, make this
curry using raw shrimp and
omit the garbanzo beans.

Swordfish Steaks

Swordfish has a firm, meaty texture, but has a tendency to dry out during cooking unless well marinated first.

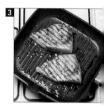

NUTRITIONAL INFORMATION

Calories	548	Sugars	.........0g
Protein	........28g	Fat	..........48g
Carbohydrate	....1g	Saturates	.......7g

2¼ hrs   4–6 mins

SERVES 4

I N G R E D I E N T S

4 swordfish steaks, about 5½ oz/150 g each

4 tbsp olive oil

1 garlic clove, crushed

1 tsp lemon rind

lemon wedges and parsley sprigs, to garnish

freshly cooked vegetables, to serve

S A L S A   V E R D E

4 anchovies in oil, drained

1 cup flatleaf parsley leaves

½ cup mixed fresh herbs, such as basil, mint, and chives

1 garlic clove, chopped

1 tbsp capers, drained and rinsed

1 tbsp green peppercorns in brine, drained

1 tsp Dijon mustard

½ cup extra-virgin olive oil

salt and pepper

VARIATIONS

Any firm fleshed-fish will do for this recipe. Try tuna or even shark instead.

1 Wash the dry the swordfish and place in a nonmetallic dish. Combine the olive oil, garlic, and lemon rind. Pour over the swordfish and marinate for 2 hours.

2 For the salsa verde, coarsely chop the anchovies and put with the other ingredients in a food processor. Process to a smooth paste, adding a little warm water if necessary. Season to taste with salt and pepper and set aside.

3 Remove the swordfish steaks from the marinade. Cook on a barbecue or preheated ridged grill pan for 2–3 minutes each side, until tender. Garnish with lemon wedges and parsley and serve with the salsa verde and freshly cooked vegetables.